HALIFAX
TASTES

Recipes from the Region's Best Restaurants
with Liz Feltham

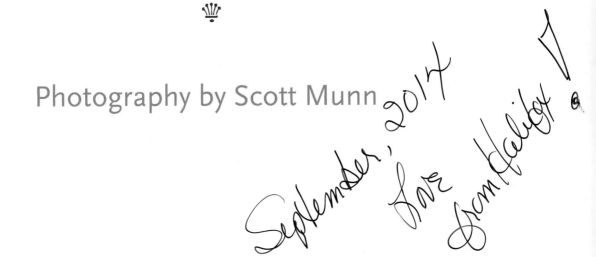

Photography by Scott Munn

September, 2017
Love
from Halifax !

NIMBUS
PUBLISHING

For madraG, whose quiet courage and fierce determination in the face of battle are awe-inspiring, and deeply humbling.

Nimbus Publishing Limited
3731 Mackintosh St, Halifax, NS B3K 5A5
(902) 455-4286 nimbus.ca

Printed and bound in China
Design: Jenn Embree

Library and Archives Canada Cataloguing in Publication

Feltham, Liz
Halifax tastes : recipes from the region's best restaurants / Liz Feltham ; Scott Munn, photographer.

Issued also in an electronic format.
ISBN 978-1-77108-006-4

1. Cooking, Canadian—Nova Scotia style. 2. Cooking—Nova Scotia—Halifax. 3. Cookbooks. I. Munn, Scott II. Title.

TX715.6.F445 2013   641.59716'225   C2012-907361-X

Nimbus Publishing acknowledges the financial support for its publishing activities from the Government of Canada through the Canada Book Fund (CBF) and the Canada Council for the Arts, and from the Province of Nova Scotia through the Department of Communities, Culture and Heritage.

table of contents

introduction

Times are good for restaurant-goers in the Halifax Regional Municipality.

HRM's food fabric has been woven into a patchwork quilt over the years: the typical Greek-owned family restaurants like the Canadiana (in its Barrington Street location), Cousins, and Athens have squares; early pioneers of fine dining—Fat Frank's Frank Metzger, Alex Clavel's Clipper Cay, and Deanna Silver's Silver Spoon have squares. Take-outs and chip trucks have earned squares: Willman's, Bud the Spud, John's Lunch.

And the fabric is shot through with ethnic threads; some, like Chinese, Italian, and Indian, are more tightly interwoven than others (like Russian, Ethiopian, and Spanish).

Ethnic cuisine began with the donair and rode a sushi tsunami, from Addis Ababa (Ethiopian) to Zorba the Greek and everything in between.

A handful of chef-owners brought early influences and continue to do so through their legacy of outstanding restaurants: Maurizio Bertossi brought Italian cooking out of the red sauce and Chianti era, first in the kitchen at La Perla and then in his namesake daMaurizio and now il Mercato, the Bicycle Thief, and Ristorante a Mano. Unni Simensen's Scandinavian way of cooking begat Scanway Restaurant, then Sweet Basil, Saege, and her flagship pastry and catering shop, Scanway Catering.

Sometime in the nineties, hotel restaurants started to shake the stigma of being just amenities for guests; Ray Bear turned Gio at the Prince George into a destination restaurant; Luis Clavel at Seasons by Atlantica and Erwin Palo at Café 101 in the Holiday Inn Harbourview compete successfully on the national level, experiment with molecular gastronomy,

and put their personal stamps on the once generic hotel restaurant standard.

Locavore, fifty-mile dining, fresh and local: all catchphrases for the trend of ethical, environmentally responsible, purist food consumption—eating food that is produced locally. Branded as a new idea but the same way our forefathers and mothers ate. A handful of chefs were doing this a decade ago: Fid's Dennis Johnston, Chives's Craig Flinn and Darren Lewis, the Halliburton's Scott Vail, all heading to the farmers' market to chat with suppliers, look for what was in season, and plan menus around the offerings.

And the neighbourhood restaurant is regaining footholds lost in the days of "everybody goes downtown to eat." Chris Smith's Jamieson's and the Christakos' Brooklyn Warehouse are two shining examples of how to do it well.

It's a great time to eat out, all right.

But with the proliferation of local fishmongers, butchers, farmer/vendors, artisan cheeses, bakeshops, and microbreweries, it's also a great time to cook at home. Which is, after all, what this book is all about—being able to recreate some of Halifax's favourite restaurant dishes right at home.

But the remarkable range and richness of offerings poses the question: Why these particular restaurants? Constrained by pages, we had to somehow cut into the culinary pie and pull out a cross-section of recipes to represent HRM. We needed to consider things geographically—not all restaurants are in the downtown core. We thought about the restaurant's lifespan, and whether or not it had a good chance of being around when the book came to print. And culinary diversity was a factor,

from family diners to fine dining and everything in between. There were some restaurants that we would have loved to include, but our invitations were declined. There are many great places that didn't make the book for one reason or another, so please don't be too upset if your favourite isn't here—a lot of our favourites didn't make it either.

Ultimately, these are the ones that did make it, and we think you'll find some recipes you like. All of these recipes have been kitchen tested, adapted for the home cook, and written to help you get the best results whether you're a cooking rookie or an old hand at the stove.

Bon appétit!

starters

Just like the preview for a movie or the back cover of a novel, the appetizer is designed to give you a hint of things to come. These starters are sure to get your taste buds warmed up and ready for the main event. Unless, of course, you decide they're worthy of being the main attraction.

hummus

MID-EAST FOOD CENTRE

The Mid-East Food Centre is the place to find any ingredients you may need to create your own feast, or enjoy the offerings of the on-site café—and whatever you do, don't skip the baklava. This hummus makes a great dip for veggies and pita chips and a healthy spread for sandwiches and wraps.

Makes about 1 1/2 cups

2 cups cooked fresh or canned chickpeas
2 cloves raw garlic
4 tablespoons fresh lemon juice
1 tablespoon tahini paste
1 teaspoon allspice
1 teaspoon cumin
1/4 cup canola oil
salt and pepper, to taste

Purée chickpeas in a food processor; add garlic and blend until smooth. Add lemon juice, tahini paste, allspice, and cumin. Slowly pour in canola oil and process until all ingredients are well mixed. Add salt and pepper to taste.

roasted beet and goat cheese salad

STORIES AT THE HALLIBURTON

A small but innovative menu fuelled by local ingredients is the hallmark of Stories' offerings. In this elegant salad, Chef Scott Vail uses local red, golden, and "candy-striped" (chiogga) beets.

Makes 4 appetizer-size salads.

Salad

- 1 pound very small unpeeled mixed beets
- 3 sprigs fresh thyme
- 2 tablespoons red wine vinegar
- 2 tablespoons olive oil
- 1/2 teaspoon salt
- 1/2 teaspoon pepper
- 1/4 pound young arugula
- 8 ounces goat cheese
- 2 ounces pistachios, peeled, roasted, and coarsely chopped

Vinaigrette

- 10 ounces fresh orange juice
- 1 small shallot, finely diced
- 2 1/2 tablespoons balsamic vinegar
- 5 ounces extra-virgin olive oil
- 1 teaspoon grated orange zest

Preheat barbecue or oven to 375°F. Divide beets according to variety (to keep the red beet colour from bleeding into the others), and lay them onto separate squares of double thickness aluminum foil. Place into each package a sprig of thyme, and drizzle red wine vinegar, olive oil, salt, and pepper over beets. Fold the edge of the foil and roll up to form a tight package.

Roast the beets on the upper rack of the barbecue or in the oven for 45 minutes to one hour, until skewer inserted into package can pierce beets with only a little resistance. Remove beets from package, allow to cool, and peel—the skins will easily slip off.

In a small saucepan over medium heat, simmer orange juice until one quarter of its original volume. Remove from heat and add diced shallot and balsamic vinegar. Slowly, in a thin steady stream, whisk in olive oil, and then add orange zest.

Dress arugula with vinaigrette and divide among the plates. Place the grilled beets around the arugula, top each salad with goat cheese and roasted pistachios, and serve.

split pea and ham soup with dumplings

EMMA'S EATERY

Kim Stacey's little diner, nestled in Eastern Passage, serves up familiar comfort food in cheery, inviting surroundings. Should you be in the Passage on a winter's day when the wind is whipping in off the water, you'll certainly appreciate the heartiness of this stick-to-your-ribs soup.

Makes 10–12 servings.

Soup

2 pounds ham bones with or without meat still attached
1 gallon cold water
1/4 cup butter
2 cups finely chopped carrot
2 cups finely chopped onion
2 cups finely chopped celery
2 cups ham chopped into bite-sized pieces
1 whole dried bay leaf
4 cups yellow split peas

Place ham bones in a large stockpot and cover with cold water. Bring to a boil, then reduce heat and simmer for at least 1 hour; liquid will reduce to soup stock consistency.

Strain ham stock into a separate pot or container and set aside. Pick any remaining meat off the bones, then discard bones.

In the stockpot over medium heat, melt butter and cook carrot, onion, and celery until tender.

Add ham stock and bay leaf and bring to a boil. Reduce heat to medium low, add split peas and simmer until peas are soft and liquid begins to thicken.

Serve with Simple Dumplings.

Simple Dumplings

2 cups all-purpose flour
4 teaspoons baking powder
1/2 teaspoon salt
3/4 cup milk

In a mixing bowl, combine flour, baking powder, and salt. Add milk and stir to make a soft dough, taking care not to over mix; dough should be airy. If dough is stiff, add a little more milk, a couple of drops at a time.

Drop dough by tablespoons into simmering soup and cover pot for 7 to 10 minutes until dumplings are fully cooked through.

signature curry lobster soup

SEASONS BY ATLANTICA

The former Holiday Inn has enjoyed a top-to-bottom makeover since it changed hands, kitchen and restaurant included. Chef Luis Clavel's beautifully complex soup is indicative of the style of cooking he has brought to the Seasons kitchen.

Makes 16 servings.

3 tablespoons vegetable oil
1 cup minced Spanish onion
1 teaspoon minced fresh garlic
1 teaspoon minced fresh ginger
3 cups diced sweet potato
2 tablespoons garam masala
2 tablespoons cumin powder
2 tablespoons coriander powder
1 teaspoon turmeric powder
1 quart tomato purée
3 quarts concentrated lobster stock*
3 cups diced fresh ripened beefsteak
   tomatoes, seeds removed
3/4 cup chopped fresh cilantro (no stems)
4 tablespoons fresh lime juice

Heat oil in large pot over medium heat; add onion, garlic, ginger, sweet potato, garam masala, cumin, coriander, and turmeric. Cook until onion and potato are softened, stirring occasionally. Add tomato purée and lobster stock and bring to boil.

After soup reaches boiling point, stir in diced tomatoes, cilantro, and lime juice. Add salt and pepper, if desired, and serve.

*Concentrated lobster stock should be homemade but can also be purchased through online gourmet markets.

smokey corn and haddock chowder

Fid Resto

*A fid is a tool used to splice rope, and chef-owner Dennis Johnston splices flavours skillfully in Fid's locally focused menu.
Here, a hint of salty from the bacon fat, smoke from the corn, chipotle heat, and peppery arugula work together beautifully.*

Makes 8 servings.

1 tablespoon bacon fat
4 tablespoons finely chopped garlic
4 tablespoons chipotle peppers in adobo
2 yellow onions, peeled and sliced thinly
2 ears of corn, shucked and lightly grilled
1 tablespoon ground coriander seed
1 quart chicken stock
1 quart heavy (35%) cream
8 ounces smoked haddock, thinly sliced
salt to taste
pepper to taste
2 cups arugula
4 teaspoons sliced green onion

In a large pot over medium heat, cook onions, garlic, and chipotle peppers in bacon fat until softened. Remove corn kernels from the cob and add to pot, stirring until heated. Add coriander seed, chicken stock, and cream. Increase heat and let simmer about 20 minutes. Process with hand blender until relatively smooth (soup may also be blended in food processor). If soup is too thick, add more chicken stock or cream until desired consistency is reached. After processing, season with salt and pepper.

To serve, place 1 ounce of smoked haddock in bottom of each soup bowl, then fill with soup. Garnish with arugula and green onion, and serve.

crab dumplings

THE PRESS GANG

"This would be a great place to take someone on a romantic date," my husband remarked during our first visit to The Press Gang. (Clearly, dinner with your wife does not count, I wryly supposed). The ambience is indeed intimate, accentuated by the oyster bar and such rich dishes as these crab dumplings.

Makes 6 servings.

1/2 cup butter
1/2 cup yellow onion, finely diced
1 tablespoon fresh garlic, finely chopped
1 tablespoon fresh ginger, finely chopped
1 tablespoon ground cumin
1 tablespoon ground nutmeg
1 tablespoon cayenne
1 pound lump crabmeat, picked over for cartilage
2 cups potatoes, mashed and slightly warm
1 whole egg
1 egg yolk
3 tablespoons fresh chervil
1/2 teaspoon salt
2 cups all-purpose flour
canola oil for frying

Melt the butter in a large frying pan over medium heat. Add onion and garlic; cook until softened but not browned. Add ginger, cumin, nutmeg, and cayenne and continue to cook 1–2 minutes. Remove from heat.

In a large bowl, mix crabmeat, mashed potato, whole egg, egg yolk, salt, and chervil. Add spice mixture from frying pan, then add flour until a soft dough is formed.

Let dough rest in refrigerator for a minimum of 30 minutes (chilling the mixture will make it easier to handle and help the dumplings keep their shape while cooking).

After chilling, roll dumplings out and cut into bite-sized pieces. In a large frying pan, heat oil over medium heat and carefully add dumplings, cooking until browned on all sides. Serve immediately.

smoked cod potato cakes with warm tomato chow

JAMIESON'S

These classic potato cakes are representative of the hearty, authentic fare of Irish pub-style Jamieson's, beloved by its patrons for great food, ale, and community spirit. Owner Chris Smith opens Jamieson's doors each Christmas Day offering free dinner for those hungry in body or soul.

Makes 12 servings.

Cod Cakes

1 pound smoked cod fillets, picked for bones
8 cups mashed potatoes, cooled (about 16 medium potatoes)*
2 tablespoons Dijon mustard
1 1/2 cups green onion, sliced (about 1 bunch)
1–2 cups bread crumbs for coating
2–4 tablespoons butter

In a large bowl, combine cod, mashed potatoes, Dijon mustard, and green onions and mix well. Divide mixture into 24 balls, forming each ball into a cake shape with your hands.

Coat cakes with thin layer of bread-crumbs. Refrigerate for 30 minutes to 1 hour before frying; this will help cakes keep their shape.

Preheat oven to 350°F.

In a large skillet over medium heat, melt butter. Add cakes to hot butter, turning once so that both sides are browned. Place fried cakes on baking sheet and place in the oven for 3 to 5 minutes to finish.

Serve, 2 cakes per serving, with Jamieson's Signature Tomato Chow.

*These can be plain or with cream and butter added.

Makes 1–1 1/2 quarts, depending on size of tomatoes.

Jamieson's Signature Tomato Chow

10 fresh whole tomatoes, cored and diced
2 cups Spanish onion, diced (about 1 large onion)
3/4 cup white sugar
3/4 cup vinegar
1 tablespoon ground turmeric
2 tablespoons ground pickling spice
salt and pepper to taste, if desired

In a large pot over low heat, combine tomatoes, onion, sugar, vinegar, turmeric, and pickling spice. Simmer until tomatoes are very tender and most of the liquid has evaporated; time will vary depending on ripeness of tomatoes.

Combine all ingredients in a medium sized pot over low heat.

Add salt and pepper to taste.

crab cakes with roasted red pepper remoulade

CELLAR BAR AND GRILL

Whether gathering around the cozy fireplace in winter or on the rooftop deck in summer, diners in Bedford have been enjoying the Cellar's diverse menu for nearly two decades.

Makes 8 crab cakes.

Crab Cakes

1 teaspoon olive oil
1 cup yellow onion, finely chopped
1 pound lump crabmeat, squeezed and
   picked through for cartilage
2 tablespoons chopped fresh parsley
1/4 cup diced red pepper
1 sliced green onion
1 tablespoon chopped canned jalapeno
2 cloves roasted garlic, puréed
1 pinch chili flakes
4 teaspoons grated lime zest (2 limes should
   give enough zest and juice for the recipe)
6 tablespoons fresh lime juice
1 1/2 cups mayonnaise
3/4 cup panko bread crumbs
salt and pepper to taste

For breading:
1/2 cup flour
2 eggs, lightly beaten
1/2 cup panko bread crumbs

Heat olive oil in frying pan over medium heat, add onion, and cook until lightly browned. Remove from heat and set aside. In a mixing bowl, combine crab meat, parsley, red pepper, green onion, jalapeno, garlic, chili flakes, lime zest, lime juice, and mayonnaise. Add panko crumbs, salt and pepper (if desired), and mix gently until ingredients hold together.

Divide crab mix into 2-ounce portions and shape into cakes. Dredge each cake in flour, then beaten eggs, then bread crumbs, then lay out on baking sheets. Chilling for at least 30 minutes at this stage will help the cakes retain their shape during frying.

Preheat deep fryer to 400°F. Fry cakes until golden brown and serve with Roasted Red Pepper Remoulade.

Roasted Red Pepper Remoulade

1 large whole red pepper
1/2 teaspoon olive oil
1/2 teaspoon salt
1/4 teaspoon pepper
1/2 cup mayonnaise
1 pinch ground ginger
2 teaspoons lime or lemon juice
1 pinch cumin
dash hot sauce

Preheat oven to 375°F. Toss red pepper with olive oil, salt, and pepper. Roast on middle rack in oven until skin is charred. Place in glass bowl and cover with plastic wrap. Let pepper sit until cooled. Once cooled, peel skin and remove seeds and white membrane.

Purée pepper in food processor, add mayonnaise, ground ginger, citrus juice, cumin, and hot sauce. Process until smooth.

mains

Seafood features prominently, as you might expect; with such fresh daily catches available practically at their restaurants' doorsteps, chefs are always creating dishes to showcase the very best the Atlantic has to offer.

And with the locavore movement on the rise, it's not just fish that producers are focusing on—Nova Scotia beef, chicken, and pork are becoming more prevalent in farm markets and grocery stores and take centre stage in some of our main courses as well.

Tess's Louisiana grill

Chez Tess

Chez Tess is nestled on a quiet side street in Halifax's North End, offering an oasis from the busy streets surrounding it. Initially known primarily for their crepes, the menu has expanded to include favourites like the Louisiana Grill.

Makes 8 servings.

250 grams penne (about 4 cups, uncooked)
1 green pepper, diced large
1 red pepper, diced large
1 small red onion, thinly sliced
2 cloves minced fresh garlic
2 tablespoons extra-virgin olive oil
2 tablespoons Cajun spice
1 pound chicken breast, cooked and sliced thin
2 andouille sausages, thinly sliced
2 cups marinara sauce
2 cups heavy (35%) cream

Preheat oven to 350°F. Cook penne according to package directions.

While penne is cooking, place peppers, onions, and garlic in a medium casserole dish, toss with olive oil and 1 tablespoon of the Cajun spice. Bake for 20 minutes.

Remove casserole dish from oven and add remaining Cajun spice, chicken, penne, sausage, marinara sauce, and cream.

Cover and continue to bake in oven for 20 minutes, until heated through, then serve.

braised beef cheeks

ELEMENTS ON HOLLIS, WESTIN NOVA SCOTIAN

Located in the Westin Nova Scotian hotel, elements on hollis has been named one of Canada's Top 5 "Local" Restaurants by Food Network Canada. In this recipe, the lowly beef cheek is used to create a dish that transcends its humble ingredients to become something truly special.

Makes 6 servings.

2 pounds beef cheeks, trimmed of fat
1 teaspoon salt
1/2 teaspoon pepper
1 tablespoon olive oil
1 whole onion, roughly chopped
1 whole carrot, roughly chopped
1 celery stalk, roughly chopped
4 sprigs fresh thyme
1 sprig fresh rosemary
8 cups beef stock
1/4 cup Pat's Preserves Merlot Jelly*
1/4 cup Pat's Preserves Fig and Grand
   Marnier Jelly*

*Pat's Preserves jams and jellies are a local brand, found at the Halifax Seaport Farmers' Market

Preheat oven to 350°F. Season beef cheeks with salt and pepper, and heat oil in a large ovenproof pot on the stove, set to high. Place beef cheeks in pot and sear until browned. Remove from pot and set aside, covered.

Reduce heat to medium and add onion, carrot, celery, thyme, and rosemary to pot. Cook for 5 to 7 minutes or just until vegetables begin to soften. Raise heat to high, and return beef cheeks to pot. Add beef stock and jellies, and bring to a boil.

Cover pot with aluminum foil and place in oven for 2 to 3 hours, until beef is very tender. Remove from oven, and allow beef to cool in liquid for a minimum of 30 minutes (at 3, the beef is refrigerated and cooled overnight in the liquid).

Remove cheeks and set aside. Strain the liquid, and discard the vegetables. In a large pan over high heat, simmer the liquid until it is reduced in volume by half. Use this liquid to reheat the cheeks just before serving.

Serve over pasta or potatoes.

huevos rancheros

THE COASTAL CAFÉ

Coastal Café chef-owner Mark Giffin thought there was a need for a casual brunch option in Halifax; if the lineups that are frequently seen out the door are any indication, a lot of other people think so too! This recipe is one of the booming restaurant's most popular brunch dishes.

Makes 2 servings.

Huevos Rancheros

4 corn tortillas, brushed with oil and baked
  until crispy
1 cup sharp cheddar
1 cup Monterey Jack
2 green onions, chopped
1 teaspoon canola oil
6 eggs
rancheros sauce (recipe below)
guacamole (recipe below)
salsa (recipe below)

Preheat oven to 350°F.

Place tortillas on a baking sheet, top each with 2 tablespoons of Rancheros Sauce, then cheddar, then Monterey Jack, then a sprinkle of green onions.

In a non-stick frying pan set at medium, heat 1/2 teaspoon canola oil.

Crack three of the eggs into a small bowl. Gently slide eggs into pan and slowly cook until whites begin to firm up. Gently flip eggs, cooking to personal preference. (Eggs may also be scrambled or poached if desired.)

Remove tortillas from oven and transfer two to a plate. Slide eggs over tortillas. Crack next three eggs and repeat for second serving.

Top with Guacamole and Salsa and serve immediately.

Rancheros Sauce

1 teaspoon canola oil
1 red pepper, chopped
1 small white onion, chopped
2 cloves garlic, chopped
2 guajillo peppers, chopped*
1 New Mexico chili, chopped*
1 can (796 ml) of San Marzano tomatoes
4 tablespoons chili powder
1/4 cup honey
dash salt
dash pepper

Heat canola oil in frying pan over medium heat. Add red pepper, onion garlic, guajillo peppers, New Mexico chili, and cook until vegetables are softened.

Add tomatoes, chili powder, honey, salt, and pepper, and bring to a boil. Reduce heat and simmer for 1 hour, then purée until smooth. This is more than you will need for one batch; the leftovers will keep refrigerated up to a week.

Guacamole

2 ripe avocadoes, diced
4 teaspoons grated lime zest (2 limes should
   give enough zest and juice for the recipe)
6 tablespoons fresh lime juice
1/2 bunch fresh cilantro, chopped
1/2 red onion, diced
1 small tomato, diced
1/2 teaspoon ground cumin
dash salt
dash pepper

Combine in one bowl avocado, lime zest, lime juice, cilantro, onion, tomato, cumin, salt, and pepper; leave chunky. Refrigerate until use.

Salsa

1 1/2 cups chopped fresh tomatoes
1/2 red onion, chopped
2 cloves garlic, chopped
1 red habanero pepper
2 arbol chilies*
4 teaspoons grated lime zest (2 limes should
   give enough zest and juice for the recipe)
6 tablespoons fresh lime juice
1/2 bunch fresh cilantro, chopped
dash salt
dash pepper

Combine tomato, onion, garlic, peppers, lime juice, lime zest, cilantro, salt, and pepper. Purée until smooth, refrigerate until use.

*This recipe uses a variety of chilies to provide depth and nuance of flavour. Guajillo peppers are dried mirasol chilies, more sweet than hot. New Mexico chilies come in green and red varieties and range in heat level. Arbol chilies and thin, red, fiery hot chilies. Habaneros are small and very intense, among the hottest of the chilies.

peach and prosciutto pizza with maple rosemary aioli

MORRIS EAST

Jennie Dobbs was serious about wood-fired pizza when she opened Morris East—she imported a wood-burning oven from Naples to ensure an authentic product. This peach and prosciutto combo is a prime example of the innovative pizzas served in the restaurant.

Makes 1 pizza (12").

Pizza

- 1 whole fresh peach, sectioned into eight wedges
- 1 Morris East pizza dough ball*
- 1 tablespoon Maple Rosemary Aioli
- 1/4 cup goat cheese
- 2 ounces microgreens or arugula
- 3 slices prosciutto
- 1 teaspoon fresh chopped rosemary (saved from aioli recipe)

Preheat oven to 350°F. Spread peach wedges on baking sheet and roast for 15 minutes or until edges start to brown.

On a pizza board or pan, stretch out dough to form a 12" circle. Top with a tablespoon of aioli and arrange peach slices and goat cheese around dough.

Bake for 15 minutes, until dough is cooked. Remove from oven, top with fresh microgreens or arugula and slices of prosciutto. Sprinkle with fresh rosemary, serve.

Maple Rosemary Aioli

- 1 egg yolk
- 1 teaspoon pure maple syrup
- 2 sprigs fresh rosemary, chopped (set aside 1 teaspoon for garnish)
- 1 cup extra-virgin olive oil
- 1 tablespoon grated lemon zest (about 1 lemon)
- 1/4 cup fresh lemon juice (about 1 lemon)
- 1 tablespoon water

In a food processor, blender, or by hand, whisk egg yolk with maple syrup and rosemary. Very slowly, in a thin steady stream, add the olive oil; you will see the ingredients thicken as they emulsify. Once emulsified, whisk in lemon zest, juice, and water.

*Morris East sells their fabulous pizza dough—white, whole wheat, or gluten-free—right in the restaurant for take-home.

baked haddock stuffed with shrimp and scallops and pernod cream sauce

ENCORE, INN ON THE LAKE

The lovely small hotel, Inn on the Lake is especially popular with wedding parties for its beautiful setting on the shores of Lake Thomas. At Encore, this baked haddock recipe is made using metal "collars" or ring moulds to keep its shape; if you don't have such moulds, the presentation may not be as precise, but the flavours will still be there.

Makes 10 servings.

Baked Haddock

12 button mushrooms, thinly sliced
1 medium carrot, julienned
2 cups baby spinach
1 small red onion, thinly sliced
1 pound baby shrimp, cooked
1 pound baby scallops, cooked
5 haddock fillets (8 ounces each), raw
2 teaspoons salt
1 teaspoon pepper

Preheat oven to 350°F. In a microwave or over boiling water, steam mushrooms, carrots, spinach, and onion just until softened. Set aside.

Cut haddock into quarters lengthwise so that you have twenty longer, narrow pieces.

Brush the inside of 10 ring molds with olive oil, line with parchment paper. Lay them on a baking sheet lined with parchment.

Rim each collar inside with 2 haddock quarters. Stuff each haddock ring with equal portions of mushroom, carrot, spinach, onion, shrimp, and scallop, season with salt and pepper.

Bake for 20 minutes, remove from oven, and remove parchment lining the baking sheet to allow cooking liquid to drain.

Serve with Pernod Cream Sauce.

Pernod Cream Sauce

4 cups heavy (35%) cream
1 cup fish stock
3/4 cup finely chopped fennel bulb (about 1/2 small bulb)
1 tablespoon cornstarch
2 ounces Pernod

Add heavy cream, fish stock, and fennel to a heavy-bottomed saucepan. Over medium heat, reduce in volume until you have about 2 cups of liquid.

Remove from heat and strain to remove fennel bits. Return sauce to pot over medium heat, add cornstarch, and stir until thickened.

Stir in Pernod and serve.

poached sea trout with sesame ginger broth

CHIVES CANADIAN BISTRO

Chefs Craig Flinn and Darren Lewis opened Chives in 2001 to almost instant acclaim. A fresh, eclectic menu focused on local ingredients that changes every six to eight weeks has kept the restaurant feeling new and never stale. This sea trout recipe, with its heavy Asian influence, is an example of the beautifully balanced flavours found at Chives.

Makes 8 servings.

1 cup dried Chinese shiitake mushrooms
4 cups low sodium fish, chicken, or
  vegetable broth
1/2 cup mirin (sweet rice wine)
1 tablespoon fish sauce
2 tablespoons low sodium soy sauce
1 tablespoon freshly chopped ginger
1 teaspoon toasted sesame oil
1/2 cup dulse (optional)
2 cloves garlic, sliced
4 small bok choy, sliced
1 red bell pepper, sliced
1 fresh red chili, seeds removed and finely
  chopped
8 ounce fresh snow peas
2 green onions, sliced
8 sea trout fillets (3 ounces each), skinned
  and deboned
8 ounces rice noodles, cooked (follow cooking
  instructions on package; some noodles are
  thicker than others and will take a couple of
  minutes, others will cook almost instantly
  on being plunged in hot water)

Prior to making the broth, hydrate the dried shiitake mushrooms in the fish stock for 30 minutes to 1 hour. Remove them when soft and cut off the tough stem just under the mushroom cap. Discard stems and slice caps into thin slices.

In a large braising pot, combine the broth, sliced shiitake mushrooms, mirin, fish sauce, soy sauce, ginger, sesame oil, dulse, and garlic, and bring to a simmer.

Add the bok choy, red pepper, chili, snow peas, and green onions. Cook for 3 or 4 minutes and then lower the heat slightly, just under the previous simmer.

Place the trout fillets in the broth and poach for 4 minutes until just cooked through.

To serve, place a mound of warm rice noodles in the bottom of eight deep soup bowls. Remove the trout from the broth using a slotted spoon or spatula, and set it on a warmed plate while dividing the broth and all the vegetables evenly into the bowls. Place the trout on top of the broth and vegetables, and serve immediately.

roasted atlantic halibut in a mushroom broth

daMaurizio

A few years ago daMaurizio changed hands, when Chef Andrew King bought it from his then-boss Maurizio Bertossi; fans of the popular Italian eatery need not have worried. Chef King has continued the tradition of superlative Italian food with excellent wines and outstanding service.

Makes 4 servings.

3 Italian sausages
4 tablespoons canola oil, divided in half
1 small Spanish onion, diced
1 cup shiitake mushrooms, stems and caps separated
1 cup button mushrooms, roughly chopped
1/2 cup dry white wine
6 cups chicken stock
1/2 cup dried porcini mushrooms
2 tablespoons thyme, chopped
8 unpeeled fingerling or nugget potatoes
4 fillets fresh Atlantic halibut (6 ounces each)
1 teaspoon salt
1 teaspoon pepper
12 Digby clams, cooked
1/4 cup cooked lima beans
12 cherry tomatoes
2 tablespoons white truffle oil
2 tablespoons chopped fresh chives

In a saucepan over medium heat, bring water to a simmer. Add sausages, poach for 10 minutes just until cooked. Drain water and set sausages aside.

Heat first two tablespoons of oil in small pot, add onion, button mushrooms, and shiitake mushroom stems. Sauté until brown, about 5 minutes.

Add white wine and simmer until liquid is reduced by half. Add chicken stock, dried porcini mushrooms, and thyme. Continue simmering for about 20 minutes; liquid will now be reduced to about 1 quart. Strain this liquid, and set aside to cool.

Boil potatoes until tender, remove from water, and cut each potato in half.

Slice sausages into 12 slices.

Preheat oven to 400°F.

Season halibut fillets with salt and pepper. Heat second measure of canola oil in a large, ovenproof skillet over high heat until oil begins to smoke. Lay halibut carefully in the hot oil, and sear until fish is golden brown, about 2 minutes. Place in oven, and bake until flaky, 7 to 8 minutes.

In a large non-stick pan over medium heat, add sausage and sauté on both sides for about 1 minute each. Slice shiitake mushroom caps and add to pan, continue cooking for 2 minutes.

Add mushroom broth, Digby clams, lima beans, cherry tomatoes, and cooked potatoes. Bring to boil for 1 minute.

Remove broth from pot and divide equally among four bowls. Place halibut atop bowls, drizzle each bowl with 1/2 tablespoon truffle oil, sprinkle with chopped chives, and serve.

pan-roasted arctic char with orange rosemary beurre blanc

THE FIVE FISHERMEN RESTAURANT AND GRILL

The Five Fishermen has a rich, colourful history; as the funeral home where victims of both the Titanic *and the Halifax Explosion were laid out, it's no wonder the restaurant is believed to be haunted.*

Makes 4 servings.

For the sauce:

2 tablespoons orange zest
1/2 cup orange juice
1/2 cup white wine
1 sprig fresh rosemary, plus 1 tablespoon chopped for garnish
2 ounces heavy (35%) cream
2 ounces butter, cold and cubed
Salt and freshly ground black pepper, if desired

In a saucepot over medium heat add orange zest, orange juice, white wine, and sprig of rosemary. Reduce to 1/2 cup of liquid. Strain and return to saucepot. Over medium heat, whisk in cream and bring to a low boil. Turn heat to low and whisk in cold cubes of butter. Remove rosemary sprig and season with salt and pepper, to taste. Set aside, and keep sauce warm while preparing the fish.

For the fish:

1/2 ounce olive oil
1/2 teaspoon salt
1/4 teaspoon black pepper
4x6-ounce fillets Arctic char, skin removed

In a skillet, heat olive oil over medium. Season fish with salt and pepper, then add to hot pan. Allow fish to cook until golden brown, about 2 to 3 minutes per side.

Remove fish from pan and place on top of warmed wild rice. Add sauce over and around fish. Garnish with chopped rosemary and orange segments, and serve.

For the plate:

2 cups cooked wild rice
1 tablespoon chopped rosemary
8 orange segments

manchego and chorizo mac 'n cheese

THE ARMVIEW

For over fifty years, the Armview Diner was a fixture near the Armdale roundabout; in 2006 it was reopened after extensive renovations. The decor pays tribute to the diner roots, while the eclectic menu sports comfort food favourites with modern twists. Here, macaroni and cheese gets the Spanish treatment with the addition of manchego cheese and chorizo sausage.

Makes 4 servings.

2 cups uncooked macaroni
2 chorizo sausages
1/2 red onion, finely diced
3 cloves garlic, minced
2 ounces dry sherry
6 ounces manchego cheese
2 cups heavy (35%) cream
4 sprigs fresh thyme, chopped
3 ounces panko bread crumbs
1 teaspoon dry oregano leaves
1 teaspoon smoked paprika
1 teaspoon garlic powder
1 teaspoon onion powder

In a large pot of boiling, salted water, cook macaroni noodles for 7 minutes or until al dente. Drain the noodles, and rinse under cold water to stop cooking. Set aside.

Preheat oven to 325°F.

Remove the sausage meat from the casings. In a frying pan over medium heat, cook sausage, onion, and garlic until sausage is completely cooked. Add sherry to pan and deglaze; that is, using a wooden spoon, swirl sherry around while loosening any sausage bits that are stuck on the pan.

Add cheese and cream, and simmer until sauce thickens, stirring frequently. Remove from heat, and add macaroni and thyme.

In a small mixing bowl, stir together panko, oregano, paprika, garlic, and onion powders. Pour the macaroni-sausage mix into an ovenproof casserole dish. Top with the panko-herb blend, and bake, covered, for 20 minutes. Uncover, and continue baking for another 5 minutes until top begins to brown.

peppered prosciutto-wrapped halibut with mango salsa

NECTAR SOCIAL HOUSE

Nectar is home to great cocktails, elegant (yet not stuffy) decor, an extensive wine list, and innovative cuisine. Chef Jeremy Mclean describes this dish, which he serves with quinoa, snow peas, and asparagus, as quick, elegant, and sure to please the eye and the palate.

Makes 4 servings.

Halibut

4 fillets fresh Atlantic halibut (6 ounces each)
2 teaspoons fresh ground black pepper
4 slices prosciutto
1 teaspoon canola oil

Preheat oven to 350°F. Season each halibut fillet with 1/2 teaspoon black pepper. Wrap a slice of prosciutto around each fillet, leaving ends of fish exposed.

In a large ovenproof skillet, heat canola oil just to smoking. Carefully add fish and sear just until browned. Place fish in oven and finish cooking, 8–10 minutes.

Serve with Mango Salsa.

Mango Salsa

1 ripe mango, peeled and diced
1 fresh jalapeno pepper, seeds removed and minced
1 tablespoon fresh lime juice

Combine mango, pepper, and lime juice in a glass bowl. Let sit at least 15 minutes to allow flavours to blend.

apple sausage cornbread-stuffed double pork chops with apple cider reduction

CAFÉ 101, HOLIDAY INN HALIFAX HARBOURVIEW

Under the expert guidance of Chef Erwin Palo, Café 101 is enjoying a new life as more than just a convenient spot to eat for hotel guests. This pork chop dish may seem complicated because everything is from scratch, but you can break it down into more manageable steps by doing things ahead of time, such as making the cornbread and reduction the day before.

Makes 6 servings.

Pork Chops

1 teaspoon salt
1/2 teaspoon pepper
6 double pork chops
1 teaspoon canola oil
4 cups Cornbread stuffing
1 cup Apple Cider Reduction

Season pork chops with salt and pepper; set aside. Heat oil in frying pan over medium heat. Sear double pork chops on both sides till golden in colour (1–2 minutes per side). Remove from heat and let cool.

Preheat oven to 400°F.

Place chops on a cutting board and slice horizontally in the middle, creating a pouch.

Stuff chops with the sausage cornbread stuffing, then brush with apple cider reduction. Place chops in a baking pan in oven, and cook about 12 minutes.

To serve, drizzle with more apple cider reduction.

Cornbread

1/2 cup all-purpose flour
1/2 cup yellow cornmeal
1/2 cup white sugar
1/4 teaspoon salt
2 teaspoons baking powder
1 egg
1 cup milk
1/3 cup vegetable oil

Preheat oven to 375°F. In a large bowl, combine flour, cornmeal, sugar, salt, and baking powder. Stir in egg, milk, and vegetable oil until well combined. Pour batter into greased 9 x 9-inch pan and bake in the oven for 20 minutes, or until a toothpick inserted comes out clean.

Apple Sausage Cornbread Stuffing

1/2 teaspoon vegetable oil
1/2 medium white onion, finely chopped
1 tablespoon minced garlic
1 1/2 pounds apple sausage, casing removed and cut into 1/8-inch thick slices
1 cup peeled diced apples
2 sprigs fresh thyme
1/4 teaspoon summer savory
1 quart apple juice
1/2 pan cornbread, crumbled

In a saucepan or sauté pan, heat oil over medium heat. Cook onion until soft, add garlic and sausages, and continue cooking until sausage is done; add apples and cook another 2–3 minutes. Stir in thyme, savory, apple juice. Toss with cornbread to mix thoroughly.

Apple Cider Reduction

1 quart apple juice
1 stick cinnamon
1 teaspoon ground nutmeg
1/4 teaspoon cayenne pepper

In a saucepan over medium heat, combine apple juice, cinnamon, nutmeg, and cayenne pepper. Simmer and reduce till liquid thickens, about 1 hour.

tuna tataki

SUSHI NAMI ROYALE

Sushi Nami Royale offers not just sushi but an extensive Japanese menu and surprises like deep-fried bananas for dessert. Buy only very fresh tuna for this tataki recipe, as it is served nearly raw and even the slightest sign of aging will be quickly apparent.

Makes 1 piece of tataki.

Tuna

3 oz high-quality fresh tuna, preferably yellowfin or bluefin
1 sheet seaweed (nori)
Tempura Batter
sesame seeds
sesame oil

Heat deep fryer to 425°F.
Wrap the tuna tightly in the seaweed, covering the fish completely.
 Dip tuna bundle in Tempura Batter and sprinkle with sesame seeds.
 Deep-fry just until batter is golden brown.
 Remove from fat and allow to cool slightly before slicing.
 Arrange slices on a plate, drizzle fish with a little sesame oil.

Tempura Batter

1 egg
1 cup ice water or sparkling water for extra lightness
1 cup all-purpose flour, sifted

In a medium mixing bowl, beat an egg until yolk and white are well combined. Add ice or sparkling water, stir. Slowly add flour, mixing very lightly just until ingredients are combined.
 For best results, prepare just before using.

mango chicken

HONG'S KITCHEN

In a city crowded with Chinese restaurants, Hong's Kitchen in Lower Sackville has carved out a well-deserved reputation based on fresh, authentic cooking. This deceptively simple dish is an excellent representation of their outstanding menu.

Makes 2 servings.

2 tablespoons canola oil
1 whole chicken breast, sliced
1/2 green pepper, sliced lengthwise in strips
1/2 red pepper, sliced lengthwise in strips
1/2 Spanish onion, thinly sliced
1 celery stalk, thinly sliced
4 ounces water
1 ounce white vinegar
2 tablespoons white sugar
pinch salt
1 fresh mango, peeled and diced

Add canola oil to frying pan and heat over medium; add chicken and stir-fry until chicken is about half cooked. Add peppers, onion, celery, and water, and continue frying until chicken is cooked through.

Once chicken is cooked, add vinegar, sugar, salt, and mango. Increase heat and bring to boil, then serve over rice.

desserts

Ever wonder why we always seem to have room for dessert?
A wise woman once told me it's because we have a separate
"dessert stomach." I completely buy that, and it will come in
handy when you're trying any of these special sweet treats.

pecan butter cake

IL MERCATO TRATTORIA

Patrons of il Mercato are greeted at the door by a show-stopping dessert case that truly makes you want to eat dessert first. This nutty butter cake satisfies the sweet tooth after a meal and also goes well with afternoon espresso.

Makes 1 cake (8").

Topping

1 cup packed brown sugar
2 ounces unsalted butter
1/4 cup heavy (35%) cream
1 cup pecan halves, toasted

Line a greased 8" springform pan with parchment paper. Combine brown sugar and butter until smooth. Mix in cream and continue to blend until smooth. Spread into bottom of pan, and layer pecans on top.

Cake

1 cup cake flour*
1 teaspoon baking powder
1/2 teaspoon salt
2/3 cup ground pecans
8 ounces soft unsalted butter
3/4 cup brown sugar
3 eggs
1 tablespoon instant espresso
1 teaspoon vanilla

Preheat oven to 375°F. In a large mixing bowl, sift together flour, baking powder, and salt, add ground pecans, and set aside.

In a second bowl, cream together butter and brown sugar until light and fluffy. Add eggs one at a time, then add vanilla and espresso.

Slowly add dry ingredients and blend just until all combined.

Pour onto pecans and topping in springform pan, bake for 40–45 minutes until skewer inserted in cake comes out clean.

*Cake flour has a much lower protein content than all-purpose flour, so will give a lighter result. If you must use all-purpose flour, use 1 cup all-purpose flour LESS two tablespoons for each cup of cake flour.

Alderney Landing
THEATRE
GALLERY
MARKET
Evan's
SEAFOOD Restaurant

kugelhopf

SCANWAY PASTRY SHOP

Professional bakeries and pastry shops, like Scanway, use weight measures for accuracy, not volume measures as most of us do at home. Best results for this fantastic lemon cake will come from using a small kitchen scale to weigh the ingredients.

Makes 1 Bundt cake.

Bundt Cake

- 340 grams all-purpose flour
- 6 grams baking powder
- 6 grams baking soda
- 1/4 teaspoon salt
- 170 grams unsalted butter, room temperature
- 340 grams granulated sugar
- 20 grams lemon emulsion
- 4 eggs, room temperature
- 375 grams sour cream
- 1 1/4 cups chopped walnuts or pecans
- 1 1/4 cups dark chocolate chips or dark chocolate chunks

Preheat oven to 375°F.

In a mixing bowl combine flour, baking powder, baking soda, and salt. Set aside.

In a separate bowl, whip together butter and sugar until light and fluffy.

In another bowl, break eggs and add lemon emulsion to the eggs (no need to beat or break yolks), then pour eggs one at a time to the butter-sugar mix, ensuring each egg is incorporated well before adding the next.

After the eggs, add sour cream and stir well, then add nuts and chocolate. Fold in dry ingredients, blending just until combined.

Spray a Bundt pan with cooking spray (or lightly grease with butter and dust with flour), and add cake batter. Bake for 40 to 50 minutes, until a skewer inserted in the centre comes out clean. Allow to cool, then drizzle with Lemon Icing.

Lemon Icing

- 1 cup sifted icing sugar
- 1 to 2 tablespoons fresh lemon juice

Stir lemon juice into icing sugar to reach desired consistency. Icing should be thin enough to drizzle without being too runny.

special scone

TWO IF BY SEA CAFÉ

Two If By Sea prides itself on outstanding coffee and baked goods, and this scone is one of their house specialties.

Makes 12 scones.

4 1/2 cups all-purpose flour
3/4 cup white sugar
1 1/2 tablespoons baking powder
1 pinch of salt
1 cup dried cranberries
1 1/2 cups white chocolate coins (Cacao Barry brand)
1/4 pound cold salted butter
2 cups buttermilk
2 to 3 teaspoons white sugar

Preheat oven to 325°F.

In a large bowl, combine flour, sugar, baking powder, and salt. Stir in cranberries, and white chocolate coins. With a cheese grater, grate cold butter into dry ingredients (butter pieces should be no bigger than peas). Pour in buttermilk.

Mix well with hands until a solid ball is formed. Dough should be neither too dry nor too sticky.

Place on lightly floured surface/counter and pat down flat until about 1 inch in thickness all over.

Using a knife, cookie cutter, or scone cutter, cut out 12 scones.

Place on parchment-lined cookie sheet and sprinkle tops with white sugar for garnish. Bake for 25 to 30 minutes, until edges start to brown.

Remove from oven, cool on cooling racks.

chocolate nemesis

BROOKLYN WAREHOUSE

Chocoholics swoon over this incredibly rich dessert. Dense flourless cake, silky mousse, fluffy pudding, all coated in chocolate: the nemesis of dieters everywhere.

Chocolate Mousse

20 ounces milk chocolate
8 ounces dark chocolate
6 cups heavy (35%) cream
12 large egg yolks
2/3 cup honey
6 gelatin sheets, bloomed*

Using a double boiler over medium heat, melt milk and dark chocolate.

In a mixing bowl, whip cream to soft peaks and set aside.

In a separate bowl, whip egg yolks to "ribbon stage" (the yolks will fall like soft ribbons back into bowl when the mixer is lifted).

In a heavy-bottomed pan over medium heat, bring honey to boil and add gelatin. Add hot honey to egg yolks and whip until light in colour and fully cooked. Add chocolate mixture to yolks. Fold whipped cream into chocolate-yolk mixture. Spread onto 3/4" baking sheet and freeze.

Chocolate Pudding

3 cups white sugar
3/4 cup cornstarch
12 large eggs
3 quarts milk
2 teaspoons vanilla extract
18 ounces softened unsalted butter
28 ounces white chocolate
6 sheets gelatin, bloomed*

*"Blooming" gelatin refers to the process of soaking it in cool liquid for 10 to 15 minutes prior to using, which will help ensure the smooth texture of the finished product. Follow package instructions for this.

In a large mixing bowl, sift sugar and cornstarch together. Add eggs and beat until smooth.

In a large heavy-bottomed pot over medium heat, bring milk to a boil and add vanilla. Add boiling milk very, very slowly into egg mixture—this is called "tempering." Adding milk to eggs too quickly will result in scrambled eggs. Once the temperature of the eggs is slowly increased, the egg mixture can be added to the milk pot.

Using a double boiler over medium heat, melt butter with white chocolate. Add the melted chocolate and butter into the milk pot.

Cook milk and chocolate mixture over medium heat until thick and bubbling, then add gelatin. Remove from heat, strain (straining removes any stringy bits of egg protein from the custard), and pour onto sheet pan. Freeze.

Flourless Chocolate Cake

20 ounces dark chocolate
12 ounces unsalted butter
10 large eggs, yolks only (set aside whites)
1 1/2 cups sugar
1 cup rice flour
2 large eggs, whites only (plus 10 whites from above)

Preheat oven to 325°F.

Line a 3/4" baking sheet with parchment paper.

Using a double boiler over medium heat, melt chocolate and butter together. In a mixer, whip egg yolks with sugar until soft peaks form. Fold egg yolk-sugar mixture and rice flour into melted chocolate. Whip egg whites until stiff peaks form, and fold into chocolate very carefully to keep the cake batter very light and fluffy.

Spread the batter over the baking sheet and bake for 15 to 25 minutes, until skewer inserted in cake comes out clean.

Chocolate Coating

2 pounds dark chocolate
1 pound unsalted butter
16 ounces canola oil

Using a double boiler over medium heat, melt chocolate, butter, and oil together, and stir until smooth. Remove from heat and allow to cool but not harden.

Assembly:

On a sheet pan, lay the flourless chocolate cake. Place the frozen Chocolate Mousse layer atop the cake, then the frozen Chocolate Pudding atop the mousse. Slowly pour the Chocolate Coating over the assembled cake. Cut into squares and serve.

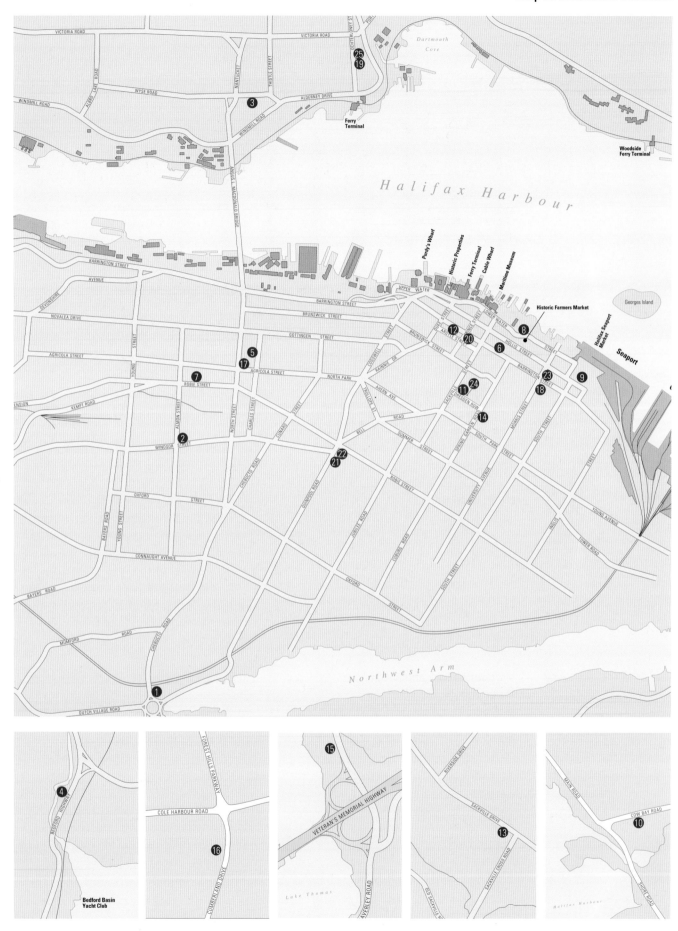

1   **The Armview**, 7156 Chebucto Road, Halifax

2   **Brooklyn Warehouse**, 2795 Windsor Street, Halifax

3   **Café 101, Holiday Inn Harbourview**, 101 Wyse Road, Dartmouth

4   **Cellar Bar & Grill**, 1516 Bedford Highway, Bedford

5   **Chez Tess**, 5687 Charles Street, Halifax

6   **Chives Canadian Bistro**, 1537 Barrington Street, Halifax

7   **The Coastal Café**, 2731 Robie Street, Halifax

8   **daMaurizio**, 1496 Lower Water Street, Halifax

9   **elements on hollis, Westin Nova Scotian**, 1181 Hollis Street, Halifax

10   **Emma's Eatery**, 31 Cow Bay Road, Eastern Passage

11   **Fid Resto**, 1569 Dresden Row, Halifax

12   **The Five Fishermen Restaurant & Grill**, 1740 Argyle Street, Halifax

13   **Hong's Kitchen**, 584 Sackville Drive, Lower Sackville

14   **il Mercato Trattoria**, 5650 Spring Garden Road, Halifax

15   **Encore, Inn on the Lake**, 3009 Hwy 2, Fall River

16   **Jamieson's**, 5 Cumberland Drive, Dartmouth

17   **Mid-East Food Centre**, 2595 Agricola Street, Halifax

18   **Morris East**, 5212 Morris Street, Halifax

19   **Nectar Social House**, 62 Ochterloney Street, Dartmouth

20   **The Press Gang**, 5218 Prince Street, Halifax

21   **Scanway Pastry Shop**, 6088 Quinpool Road, Halifax

22   **Seasons by Atlantica**, 1980 Robie Street, Halifax

23   **Stories, The Halliburton**, 5184 Morris Street, Halifax

24   **Sushi Nami Royale**, 1535 Dresden Row, Halifax

25   **Two If By Sea Café**, 66 Ochterloney Street, Dartmouth

RESTAURANT GUIDE

The Armview

manchego and chorizo mac 'n cheese

Landmark diner featuring classic diner favourites with a modern twist

7156 Chebucto Road, Halifax

902 455 4395

thearmview.com

Brooklyn Warehouse

chocolate nemesis

Neighbourhood restaurant with varied local menu

2795 Windsor Street, Halifax

902 446 8181

brooklynwarehouse.ca

Café 101, Holiday Inn Harbourview

apple sausage-cornbread stuffed pork chops

Diverse, modern menu with international influences

101 Wyse Road, Dartmouth

902 463 1100

hiharbourview.ca

Cellar Bar & Grill

crab cakes with roasted red pepper remoulade

Neighbourhood restaurant emphasizes pizzas, pastas and great wine

1516 Bedford Highway, Bedford

902 835 1568

cellarbarandgrill.ca

Chez Tess

tess's louisiana grill

Seasonal, local, with vegetarian and gluten-free options

5687 Charles Street, Halifax

902 406 3133

cheztess.ca

Chives Canadian Bistro

poached sea trout

Fresh, local, seasonal; seafood-centric

1537 Barrington Street, Halifax

902 420 9626

chives.ca

The Coastal Café

huevos rancheros

Breakfast and brunch in a relaxed, casual atmosphere

2731 Robie Street, Halifax

902 405 4022

thecoastal.ca

daMaurizio

roasted atlantic halibut

Exquisite Italian food and wine in elegant surroundings

1496 Lower Water Street, Halifax

902 423 0859

damaurizio.ca

elements on hollis, Westin Nova Scotian

braised beef cheeks

Seasonal menu with local ingredients adhering to "fifty-mile dining" philosophy

1181 Hollis Street, Halifax

902 496 7960

elementsonhollis.ca

Emma's Eatery

split pea and ham soup

Cozy community restaurant with homestyle breakfast, brunch, and lunch

31 Cow Bay Road, Eastern Passage

902 406 0606

emmaseatery.ca

Fid Resto

smokey corn and haddock chowder

Local, sustainable, regularly changing menu in casual environment

1569 Dresden Row, Halifax

902 422 9162

fidresto.ca

The Five Fishermen Restaurant & Grill

blackened haddock

Fine dining with seafood heavy menu and extensive wine list

1740 Argyle Street, Halifax

902 422 4421

fivefishermen.com

Hong's Kitchen

mango chicken

Authentic Chinese cuisine in casual surroundings

584 Sackville Drive, Lower Sackville

902 864 2897

hongskitchen.com

il Mercato Trattoria

pecan butter cake

Authentic Italian trattoria, fantastic dessert case

5650 Spring Garden Road, Halifax

902 422 2866

il-mercato.ca

Encore, Inn on the Lake

baked haddock

Casual fine dining, varied menu, lakeside patio

3009 Hwy 2, Fall River

902 861 3480

innonthelake.com

Jamieson's

potato cod cakes

Neighbourhood pub/restaurant, Irish comfort food and regional specialties

5 Cumberland Drive, Dartmouth

902 433 0500

jamiesons.ca

Mid-East Food Centre

hummus

Casual dine-in or take-out, Middle Eastern food and market

2595 Agricola Street, Halifax

902 492 0958

mideastfood.ca

Morris East

peach and prosciutto pizza

Gourmet thin-crust pizzas baked in wood-fired oven imported from Naples

5212 Morris Street, Halifax

902 444 7663

morriseast.com

Nectar Social House

prosciutto-wrapped halibut

Casually elegant wine bar with varied menu

62 Ochterloney Street, Dartmouth

902 406 3363

nectardining.com

The Press Gang

crab dumplings

Formal dining in historic surroundings, diverse menu, and signature oyster bar

5218 Prince Street, Halifax

902 423 8816

thepressgang.net

Scanway Pastry Shop

kugelhopf

Fine pastries and sweets (don't miss Unni's Famous
Florentines), distinctive cakes

6088 Quinpool Road, Halifax

902 425 6803

scanwaycatering.com

Seasons by Atlantica

curry lobster soup

Modernist cuisine in up-casual atmosphere

1980 Robie Street, Halifax

902 490 3331

seasonsbyatlantica.com

Stories, The Halliburton

roasted beet and goat cheese salad

Regional menu with focus on game and seafood

5184 Morris Street, Halifax

902 444 4400

storiesdining.com

Sushi Nami Royale

tuna tataki

Fine Japanese dining, authentic and fusion cuisine

1535 Dresden Row, Halifax

902 422 9020

sushinami.ca

Two If By Sea Café

special scone

Superior coffee, decadent pastries, and monthly "family
dinners"

66 Ochterloney Street, Dartmouth

902 469 0721

twoifbyseacafe.ca